Dedication

I dedicate this to my grandma, who was my hero, to my dad, who was my rock, and to all the special people in my life who have helped me in one form or another.

GOD'S PATHWAY

DISCOVERING THE LIFE OF *Freedom*

D.M. PRESTON

DISCOVERING THE LIFE TO FREEDOM
Copyright © 2020 by D.M. Preston

Editorial Note: All rights reserved. Contents may not be reproduced in whole or part without the express written consent of the publisher. No parts of the manual may be reproduced, stored in a retrieval system, or transmitted in any form or by any means—electronically, mechanically, photocopied, recorded, scanned, or other—except for brief quotations in critical reviews or articles, without the prior written permission of the publisher.

Unless otherwise indicated, all scripture quotations, references and definitions are from the Authorized King James Version © 1987; The New King James Version © 1982 by Thomas Nelson, Inc.; The New International Version 1973, 1978, 1984 by International Bible Society by the Zondervan Corporation; The Amplified Bible Old Testament © 1962, 1964, 1965, 1987 by the Zondervan Corporation; The Amplified New Testament © 1954, 1958, 1987 by the Lockman Foundation; The Message. Copyright © 1993, 1994, 1995, 1996, 2000, 2001, 2002.

D.M. Preston
cherish.dd64@gmail.com
214-326-5033 | www.eaglesiti.org

ISBN # 978-1-949826-19-7

All rights reserved

Published by: EAGLES GLOBAL Publishing | Frisco, Texas
In conjunction with the 2019 Eagles Authors Course
Cover & interior designed by DestinedToPublish.com | (773) 783-2981

Acknowledgments

I want to thank everyone who helped guide me through the steps of getting this book together. To my friend Terry who has passed. I did go through with writing this book. It got completed my friend we did it. And to my family, for understanding that this needed to be written to help those who can overcome or who think they can't move forward in life.

GOD'S PATHWAY

Contents

Dedication i

Acknowledgments iii

CHAPTER ONE   Living Life in Freedom 1

CHAPTER TWO   Being Abused......................................7

CHAPTER THREE   Grandma...19

CHAPTER FOUR   My Dad...25

CHAPTER FIVE   Rejection..34

CHAPTER SIX   Sacrificing..38

CHAPTER SEVEN   Desire of Living................................47

CHAPTER EIGHT   Letting Go of My Mother 52

CHAPTER NINE   Moving Forward 60

CHAPTER TEN   Seasons...65

CHAPTER ONE

Living Life in Freedom

When you grow up in a whirlwind of stuff, you might wonder how my story can connect with readers like you. I pray you find this very interesting and continue to read this book without thinking, "What is she doing?" I pray you find as you continue reading, it will help you, or you may be able to use what you have read to be a blessing to someone else.

No matter where your life takes you, whether it's upside down or right side up, we all experience life differently. Some of us have really great parents and siblings, while others wonder why we were born to the parents we were given, or why your parents acted in a certain way or did the things they did.

My life living on a roller coaster was more than I could handle, honestly. But I never let it kill me—or did I? My parents never stopped me from going to church as a kid, and that's one thing that I am so happy about. I grew up to be productive in life, and the reason behind it was because of my dad always instilling in me and my other siblings that no man would get you what you ever wanted in life. It wasn't just said to us girls, it was told to the boys as well. Maybe for the boys in the home, it was meant to give them an understanding that they should treat their women well. I really lived on that, knowing that I wanted more than I ever had as a child growing up. Did I really dislike my childhood that much in terms of how my parents raised me, or not?

Growing up, my life was not all bad I really had great moments that I would not change for the world. At times, going to visit my grandma in the nursing home, I really felt like I was on a roller coaster because I would always get so sick from the roller coaster road we took to get there. I never, ever thought that I would someday write a book about a roller coaster life by any means, but I knew God had great plans for me. I have a great time on roller coasters—I really love riding them for the thrill, even though it lasts just a small amount of time. But a lifelong journey of a roller coaster really is so different than most I have ridden.

At the church I was attending, I was invited to attend a ladies' group since I was single, though the group included married ladies as well. It was a small group, and it had its challenges, but it turned out to be a really great experience. We prayed, did many different Bible studies from many different authors, and did food carry-ins "In between Bible studies."

We helped one another if someone was in need, and we did our best to put our needs out there so one or many could help each other out. If anyone from the ladies' group happens to be reading this, know I love you all. We have changed many times with new faces. I never knew just how much baggage one person can carry throughout one's life until I got involved with this amazing group of people.

In this group, I found that doing the Breathing Free workbook by Beth Moore set the stage for me coming out and living life. I really didn't understand the whole concept of what I was about to endeavor on or endure, but I sure did go through things I had never experienced in my life. In the Bible studies we did—and still do weekly as a group of ladies—many studies have multiple weeks, and you have homework to do in between meetings. It's all personal unless you wish to share something that stuck out to you. Our group has done many studies by other Christian women; they are all different and don't hit all of us in the same way. They give us all different perspectives because we experience different things in life. But you also get out of the studies what you put into them.

As I continued through life, my favorite quote in the Bible was "Do unto others as you would want them to do unto you." I want you to know that no matter how our lives go, we are still loved unconditionally. Toward the end of one of our Bible studies, I found out that the guy I was dating was cheating on me. So, I had to go ask some questions as to why this was happening now, and I realized it was so I could move forward in the study. Had I been informed of this before I had gotten past that chapter, I would have been able to add it into the topic I was in at the time, because it would have let me forgive that too. Not that I haven't forgiven, but I have prayed for them too. I believe the more things that are given to us to deal with the stronger we are, so then we are better to able to handle it.

As time goes on, we experience things we don't think we can do, like forgive the dead. Why? Because you can't talk to them anymore. Or can you? In my experience, you can be freed from anything that has happened to you in your life when you're ready to accept it. I think you have to be in the right kind of mindset too. But who am I to say all this because it happened to me? You may have wondered this too, whether or not you have experienced something like it yourself. Each of us go through life riding our own roller coaster, and the one set forth for my life was surely one to ride.

Have you ever driven down the road crying and talking to yourself? Let me tell you, that was me one afternoon on a nice sunny day. Did I understand why and what for? Well, talking to yourself is a way to beat it all off. I knew people thought I was crazy, but it set me up for a new mindset.

I will tell you that I was shocked to find that there has been peace in my life since that day. Maybe when you listen to your inner thoughts when it's quiet, you think, "Am I really hearing what I am hearing?" You question yourself as to what you were told or heard, or what to do with your newfound thoughts. Have you ever questioned your own thoughts from time to time? Ever wonder if you had done this or that, things would have had a different outcome? It may be a possibility.

Jesus told me, "If you ever want to see me, you have to forgive your mother!" "What?" I said. "How can I do that? She's dead." A little voice said, "Just do it," and as you get to know my book, you will understand how I would say this. At the time, it bothered me, and so I went into forgiveness, crying as I went down a very busy street. People were looking at me strangely, probably wondering why I was crying. So, after praying, crying, looking stupid, I thought, "How is this really going to work? She is dead and I can't talk to her." Oh, the possibilities.

I learned to live my life in freedom while riding that roller coaster. I learned to follow my sense of not wanting to live in the past but in the freedom that I found.

The story just doesn't end until you get rid of the enemy that kept you away from your relationships with those close to you. An example is when someone wants to put a distance between you and someone you love, so there is no talking or telling about the ride you travel on. We each have to find our own way of adjusting to the abuse we have endured on our roller coaster ride. Maybe your roller coaster has been different, since our lives aren't the same, but I hope this resonates with you.

Do you have any idea of what your ride has been like, or were you always living freely? Did you find yourself on a roller coaster, wondering when it might end?

_____

_____

_____

_____

_____

_____

_____

_____

_____

_____

_____

_____

_____

_____

_____

_____

_____

CHAPTER TWO

Being Abused

As children, when we're growing up and learning what life is all about, and being still so small, we try and figure things out for ourselves, wondering what this world is all about. For me, I knew growing up that I was not my mom's favorite. Even though your parents aren't supposed to have a favorite, as a kid, you may wonder why you aren't loved or why you are being treated the way you are. I know I wasn't a good kid all the time—we all make mistakes growing up. I am not sure how you and your mother were when you were a kid, but for me, I ended up hating my mother. For you, maybe it was someone else in your life: dad, grandma, grandpa, or just someone you just wanted a closeness with.

My mother was always mistreating me so I was always in trouble with my mother all the time no matter what I did or didn't do. I would not have had to be protected by other people in my family. No matter what I did I could not make her happy. One day when I was in preschool, I got off the bus and my parents were not home. We lived in the country, and in the sixties, it wasn't abnormal to do that, or so I thought. The house was unlocked for me, and I thought it would be nice to mop the kitchen floor. Now, you have to remember that I was three or four years old at the time this all happened.

So, my parents returned home from taking my brother to the doctor. They entered the house, and oh my, she yelled at me because of what I had done by mopping the floor. I had left too much water on the floor. I guess being that age, I thought I was doing a good thing; boy, was I wrong. My dad dried up the floor and my mom whipped my butt for doing the mopping. My dad didn't really respond to her actions against me; he just did what she should have done, which was to just mop up the water and explain things. She didn't do that at all. As years went on, she wanted me to do things around the house. Well, I was never going to do it right, so I refused. Was this a problem? Of course it was. I was defiant as to what was about to continue to happen to me.

The time came when we moved from the country into town. My brother and I had the same cars and trucks that we played with—I was a tomboy—and I had to leave my purple dune buggy behind because my brother had torn his up. We were arguing and I was heartbroken, so that put a sour spot in my heart yet again for my mother.

Of course, many things had happened during this time in my life. You always can't remember all the twists and turns that were thrown at you when you were that young. But what I do remember is that it was so difficult to think about how anyone could love their mom. I began hating her at a very young age, and it wasn't all about when or why I got into trouble, because we all have to learn things. I do know she wasn't treated like that growing up. I know she wasn't wanted by her real parents, but that was not my fault.

As I continued to get older as a child, now living in town from our move from the country, my mom was a stay-at-home parent while my dad worked. But then one would wonder if she ever did anything around the house. My dad had to use his vacation time to clean the house, or we were going to be taken by Child Protective Services. My mom ended up having six kids over the years.

I kept things inside a lot over the years. I was still a young girl in elementary school—I don't want to brag, but I went from Head Start, skipped kindergarten and went straight into first grade, so it wasn't like I was a young dumb kid. As I continued through my years in elementary school. My dad had gotten hurt actually by his own nephew. It put him in the hospital for thirty days or more for a head injury. They allowed us kids to see him before they transferred him to another hospital up north. My dad was never the same after that he lost his hearing his job and much more. I can say we all lost in the process.

Dad had gotten out of the hospital during the day while we were in school and because of being away for so long he decided to go fishing that same day. On this one day we got out of school early but mom had forgotten we would get out earlier, so she thought she had plenty of time to do what she wanted. I saw her going up the street toward the store, and I had a quarter and wanted to get a pop, so I started running up the street, and she told me to go back home. I didn't listen, so she was three-fourths of the way up the street and I kept following her. When she was that far, she yelled at me to come on, so I ran to catch up with her.

When we arrived at the store, a man in a really big car was sitting in the lot. My mother walked up to the car while I remained on the sidewalk. Then she yelled at me to come over to the car, so I did. I was told to go inside and purchase a pack of gum for this man. I did as I was told, and when I returned outside, she was sitting in the front passenger seat. She told me to get in. I refused, but that didn't work very well either, so I got in the back seat of the car.

As we went up the street, I was told I was going to be dropped off at the hot dog shop to go inside and get myself a soda and hot dog, and they would be back to get me. He started out wanting to give me fifty cents, but by the time we got there, I ended up with a dollar and seventy-five cents. So, I got out and went inside the little shop, and then I waited till they left, exited the building, and headed home, crying all the way because I was so nervous about whether I was going in the right direction, and I knew I was going to be in for a beating from my mom because I didn't follow her orders.

When I made it home, my dad was there with my aunt Elizabeth. They were trying to figure out why my mom wasn't with me, considering my aunt was watching the other children until she got back from the store. So, I told them what they did and told me to do, which made them upset. Then, all of a sudden, I heard them say she was coming up the street.

Well, at this point, I knew I was in big trouble for telling and for not staying at that small shop. My father had gotten a new washer and dryer, and we were donating stuff we didn't need or couldn't wear anymore. As my mother got closer to the house, I got inside one of the boxes and covered up with many clothes and other things. Oh, after they were done drilling her, she came straight to my room, I held my breath for what seemed like forever. She sat on my bed and said, "I know you're in here. You just need to come out and get what you deserve." To me, I didn't deserve anything that was coming from her. My mother went on for some time, and I refused to move or say anything because I knew I had been had. She finally got tired, and she got up and said, "You will pay for this." All I could think was "What will she do?"

Some time later, my aunt Elizabeth came into my room and said, "You can come out, she's gone now." I waited a bit to make sure it wasn't a game and finally, I appeared. When my mom laid eyes on me again, if looks could kill, I would not be here to tell this. I was finally able to breathe air again, but it was horrifying.

The issues continued, and you will read about more later in other chapters of the book, as this roller coaster hasn't ended yet. I did my best to try and get love from her, even doing things without her asking. It then became me taking her role in life as a mom. It became my responsibility to make sure my brothers and sisters were bathed at night. When school was in session, I was to make sure they did their homework and any work from the day that never got finished. That all became my duty. My punishment was now taking care of her responsibility: her kids. I was getting older, and many things were going on in the family. I think my mother was really jealous of me and felt that I was a threat to her.

One day, my dad decided we needed to go the store and get groceries, so I went in the store with my mother. We always had to hold the cart, keep our hands to ourselves, and not touch anything. Well, guess what—one of my dad's friends was in the store, and he told my mother I was getting to be better looking than her. "That was not good," I thought.

When we returned home from the store and put everything away, my life turned upside down. She cut my bangs about an inch from the scalp. I have a long forehead, so it did not look great at all. I felt awful about how it changed my looks, and she still made me go to the school concert that evening. I hated every minute I was there because I looked so stupid in a light blue dress with lace on it and long, dark brown hair with short bangs. The twist is still coming as I continue to tell the story of my life with her.

My mother never got any simpler. I have no clue if she was blackmailing someone or doing something with someone other than my dad. After the first man, I would hope she knew that she was only spiraling downhill. When I was ten, she left my dad and us six kids. She moved in with one of her nieces, who wasn't the happiest person because she liked men. My mother started acting younger than she was. In today's society, she would be classified as a person who stood on a street corner—that is, a hooker.

When my older brother and I found out where she was, we ventured out to find out where the address was and we looked her up. She wasn't happy with us for showing up. We knocked on the door to the apartment, and we got yelled out for being there. Oh, the way they were living was a shocker. I asked to use the bathroom, and I had to go out of the apartment, down the hallway to get to the bathroom. It was a shared bathroom with everyone in the apartment complex. I really didn't want to use it, and I was told that when they used the tub, they bleached it. I wondered why anyone would go through this.

My mother came home about two weeks later, but not without issues. The men were calling her now at the house, so we were not allowed to answer the phone, but since my dad had lost his hearing, he didn't know it was men calling her.

When you're a kid, you shouldn't know these things, especially about how she treated my father during his illness. I don't know why she ever returned, and I had even told her that too. My famous name was "little BITCH." It was all so wrong. As I got older, I was able to understand her demeanor.

There was a hole in the wall next to my bed, and that's where I deposited my hair that she would pull out of my head when she snatched me up by the hair. I was so annoyed with her, and feelings of love toward her never surfaced in all my years growing up. No matter how smart I was in school and how much I accomplished, I was never good enough. I just think I reminded her so much of herself that she hated me. (The difference is that I know she didn't do well in school.) I never heard or was shown love from her. It never changed, and I always wondered, "Why?"

I am just so thankful that other family members were there to step in from time to time to stop my mother's abuse of me. I can't stop there, though, because I was also being violated as a young girl by my uncle Al (my dad's sister's husband, so he married into the family).

My aunt Elizabeth was a sweet lady, and she would ask if I would like to come out and copy recipes she wanted to keep and file and rotate her kitchen food by dates. Of course, it got me away from the house with my mom. But then, one Easter, she called and asked if I was going to be doing anything, I said no, and she said, "Well, do you want to come to the house?" Of course, I said yes. My aunt Elizabeth said, "I will have your uncle Al pick you up after work." Of course, it was dark by the time he got off work, so I had to wait for him. My uncle Al picked me up and boy was I in for a shock of a lifetime. I knew where my cousins lived, which was where we were supposed to be heading to pick my aunt Elizabeth up, and it was not in the direction we were going. After he had been driving for a while, the roads he took got me lost. I asked my uncle Al, "Where are we going?" He said we were going to his daughter's house. Well, it was nowhere I had ever been, so I questioned it, and that was wrong, because now I was being ordered to move over next to him.

Of course, I questioned why, but as a kid you are told to obey adults. After some time, he stopped the truck and pulled me next to him. I didn't understand what was happening at first, but then he put his hands down my pants and I became confused as to why he was doing this. I questioned yet again, and he said, "You know." I said, "No I don't." We argued, and while he parked off the side of the road in an area I was unfamiliar with, he told me to come with him. Of course, I refused, but nothing I was doing was changing his mind.

Then he said we were going to the back of the camper that fits on the truck beds. It was something they would park in town next to our house. Well, then here he came, taking my clothes off. I was crying and saying, "What are you doing?" His reply was "You know all about this," and I kept saying, "No I don't." I didn't understand what he was referring to until much later. Well, he took advantage of me, and I was so distraught about all the actions and hurt I felt along with the confusion. Then he told me to get dressed and sit at the table. He went into the small bathroom, and when he came out, he told me to go in there and clean up. Still lost, I did what I was told.

We finally got back on the road and headed to get my aunt Elizabeth from my cousins' house. I knew my aunt was pissed that it took us forever to get there—she was questioning his actions as to why we were late. He used the excuse that it took longer at work than he'd thought. Of course, that wasn't why he was late; it was what he did to me. My aunt didn't know that at the time, but she loved me, and she knew things were never the same.

As I mentioned before, it was Easter, so it was springtime. We arrived at my cousins' house, and their children were trying to get the festivities started with the Easter baskets. Then they persuaded their parents to give them their baskets so their grandparents would get a chance to see what they had gotten. Their parents agreed, and all I wanted to do was to go home. So the kids were excited, and I was too.

My cousins were sharing their stuff, which is always nice because we were taught to do those things out of respect for others. They asked my uncle Al (their grandpa) if he would like a jellybean. He said yes, but he told them to put it in his mouth because he didn't want to touch it. Oh, how my aunt Elizabeth came unglued! She said, "If he wants it, he can put it in his own mouth." I thought, "Oh, what is going on now?"

The kids and I retreated to their room upstairs, which had a window open to the living room. As we went upstairs, I convinced my cousins to ask if I could spend the night. They did, so I didn't have to leave with my aunt Elizabeth and uncle Al, praise God. The next day came, and they took me home. I told my mom we needed to talk; she said, "After they leave."

I finally was able to talk to my mom about what happened, and all she could say to me was "Don't be in the same room with him alone." I said, "How is that going to work? How would I explain that?" From then on, if my aunt Elizabeth wanted me to stay, I would have to have been at their house already from my parents, or it wouldn't happen. So, one day I was there, and I agreed to stay the night and do the things for her because her grandchildren weren't interested in doing them. I was in the tub bathing when my uncle Al opened the door. I screamed, and she came unglued on him, saying, "You knew she was in there getting a bath." He responded, "I forgot." She said, "How did you forget that? You knew she was here."

The argument between them stopped after a while. I finished up and went to the living room, and I knew she saw the scared look on my face. I was never asked to spend the night again—I do believe she knew something had happened and never wanted me to go through it again. I was always wondering if he had ever touched his daughters or grandkids and that is why they never stayed with them, parents protecting their own children from the abuse of their father.

When I turned 18, I exposed this to my aunt Elizabeth in front of my uncle Al down the hill from where we lived in the country. He said, "She doesn't know what she's talking about," and I gave the information about what took place on that Easter weekend. Now the war was on between them, because my aunt knew I wasn't lying. Life continued to get worse for me after I exposed his actions.

The next chapters will follow into other areas of my life. This story ends when the roller coaster stops. But I think others who were in my life as I grew up, even though they didn't go through this part of that roller coaster with me, loved me unconditionally, and they would have been by my side if they had known. Life continues to move forward into other areas no matter your age. The most important people to me as a young kid were my dad and my grandma, and you'll read about them next.

Reflections

Think of a memory from your past, whether good or bad. What was it?

_____
_____
_____
_____
_____
_____
_____
_____
_____
_____
_____
_____
_____
_____
_____
_____
_____

CHAPTER THREE

Grandma

This lady was my hero as a kid, even though she may not have heard that from me, since she passed while I was still a little girl. There is no doubt she knew it, but I don't ever remember telling her so. School had been released for the day I had come home and my grandma was gone to her daughter's house and that upset me because we were so close that she didn't share that with me. The lack of understanding adults as a child was complicated to say the least. I was so devastated when she passed. I was allowed to attend her funeral due to my closeness with her, and it helped that there was no one to watch us kids. I really gave my family and hers a run for their money, because I took off like a lightning bolt when they told us it was time to leave.

I was so upset that I came back with "I am not leaving her!" I was told to come on, and I took off running into a field. I didn't understand the concept as a very young girl of not ever being able to see her again, or even the thought of missing my grandma, but I knew I didn't want to leave her. I may have not understood things about the death of a person, let alone my grandma. But some things just happen to us in life that changes our perception of what we understand as we grow in our lives. Later in life I believe she went there knowing she wasn't going to be coming back to the house with us due to her illness had gotten worse for her.

This lady raised my mom, and we called her Grandma. My mother was left outside in a laundry basket outside my grandfather's house, so she took her in and raised her. That family was her family now. My grandma was a very lovely lady. I guess I could say she was fair, but I can't say for certain because I was not alive when she was raising my mother. But due to my own experiences, I could not see her mistreating my mother.

I didn't have any others, but she was there for me when Dad worked. I knew her love for me was something special in my family, maybe because of the abuse she had seen my mother do to me. I wish she had lived longer so I could have an answer to this, but she was eighty-eight years old (young) when she passed, so it was her time to go, to be free from her pain and health issues, but she was loved. I know she did things in her life for all of us out of respect when she would go stay with her other children. I was heartbroken the day they told me that my grandmother had passed. I even questioned, "Then why did she go stay at her daughter's?" Well, she knew I would not be able to handle the loss of her. They said Grandma had gone to a better place, that she was in no pain or despair.

To tell you a bit about why I think this is, it's because when I was having a birthday, she gave me five dollars and the other kids only got a dollar or two, which made my mom mad. No matter what the amount was, that was a huge deal of money in the sixties and seventies.

I know my grandma was fair to all her children. I grew up with her having a disease called TB (tuberculosis), a deadly disease of the lungs that causes many issues. My grandma spent a lot of time in the nursing home as we grew up. When she was well, she stayed with us; when she wasn't well, she was with other family members or in the nursing home.

She was my protector and my loving grandma who is so missed today, but I know she still looks over me daily. My cousin on my mother's side even told one of my other siblings years after my mother's death about how she would say, "Leave her alone"—"her" being me—"she wasn't doing anything wrong." They said my grandma would have me get behind her lying in bed so my mother would leave me alone. She would even ask my mother, the daughter that she raised, "Why are you doing this to your daughter? She hasn't done anything to you to get punished."

If others saw this, why did it continue and not stop the pain I was in as a child? When I could, I would go stay with my grandma when she went to her other children's houses or when she decided to try and live on her own with her condition, even though TB is highly dangerous to the people that come in contact with it. We normally have several heroes as children, and she was mine.

The older we get, the more we realize that we all leave this world at some point. We learn that the road is very hilly and has many bumps along the way, and it upsets the stomach one way or the other. While my grandma was still with us, she would read the Bible to me, even though I still didn't understand a lot about life and the things we learn as we get older. She passed one spring in the early seventies from her illness.

Dad and Grandma got along so well that she so approved of my dad with my mom. I really could not understand this, but it was their relationship, and the photos of them together make me smile. I wish that as we all mature and move through the world, things would seem to come together in each stage of life. My mom changed so much after grandma died, which I don't understand, because she was loved by her as well.

As a child, close to being a teenager I was introduced to my mother's biological mom, the woman who actually gave birth to her. She and my grandpa, as we were told at that time, came to visit with us in town. Of course, we were excited because they lived out of town, but it was nice to finally meet them. I have no clue when my mom had actually found out about her and who she was, for that matter. The two of them began writing often to stay in touch. She lived in Georgia and Florida when we were growing up, and they would come see us once in a great while, but the next time I can remember seeing them was when I was 16 years old.

When my mom died, my grandmother, her real mom, came to help my dad out with the kids who were still at home. I am not sure why she came, but at least she tried to help my dad out some. Truthfully, he really didn't have time to grieve his wife proper, and she decided to stay at the house. I am not completely sure what was going on, but one day I arrived at the house, and he told me she had to go or he was going to throw her out. I had to have the conversation with her even though I wasn't there. Because I worked, of course, and I lived in a different place. I always wondered if he disliked her because of what had happened to my mom when she was so small.

We were told we had half aunts and uncles, and one was around my age. Yet we were never mistreated by her or any of Mom's biological other siblings. When my mother's biological mom passed away, I got to meet my mother's other side of the family, and it was nice that they wanted to see us as well. Not all of us six kids were able to attend the service, but just the three girls.

I have spoken to them since, and I go visit my mom's sister and her family the most. I love them and appreciate what I have learned from her in regards to how her mom was. She said her dad always told them that her mother treated them the best she knew, on the other hand, she left them when they were kids as well. I believe my mom was more like her biological mom than like my grandma, who raised her as her own.

My aunt Mary and I have talked quite a bit about her mom and mine. She grew up almost the same way I did, having to care for her siblings and their children at a young age while her mother did what she wanted to do in life. It's amazing to me how my aunt Mary life and mine are molded almost the same. I tell her all the time, "Well, at least we know we can't deny each other," and laugh. Even our health issues are similar, though we do have some that are different because of genetics. We sure learn a lot about each other when we talk. Her husband (my uncle Jeff) says, "You can tell you two are related." We laugh at him, but it's so true.

I love them without condition, even though I wonder why some are jealous of our relationship, because they grew up around them and I was in my late forties before I ever met them. As we continue going up the hills—or better yet, going down the hills—we go forth knowing how each person plays a part in our lives.

Reflections

Losing a loved one who's special to us brings many feelings. How has this affected you? If you haven't had that experience, how do you think you would handle such a loss?

CHAPTER FOUR

My Dad

After my grandma died when I was a kid, my dad became my rock. My dad and grandma got along great—normally people have issues with the mother-in-law, but he didn't at all. While he was my rock, he was also a very hard worker. Dad provided for his family in more ways than one. As some would say, he was a jack of all trades. He was such a good person that he would give the shirt off his back to anyone who needed it. Since my father was a very hard worker, I am positive that this is where I got my drive. He never knew a stranger. Now, I try to understand what made these two opposites work, that being my mother and father. My thoughts on this matter were one sided, but they have developed over time.

He taught his children many things in life, like how to create a garden—how to get the soil ready to plant, weed it, and take care of it. When we were young, he took us into the woods around our local area, even if it was a state park, and showed us what to look for as we walked around. He talked to us about smells and sounds to watch out for while in the woods because of the deadly snakes in our area. With Dad, he would stand his ground as to what we were doing and where we were going in the woods. He didn't want us too far away from him, just in case we happened to get lost.

Dad explained to us what different roots were. He would give us their names, what to look for when finding them, and how to properly remove them from the ground without tearing the leaves off the roots. The plants had names like blood, yellow root, etc., and he told us the purpose they were used for, when to harvest them, and how to get the best from them when you knew how to clean and wash them. We went mushroom hunting in the spring when they popped up out of the ground. At one point, we sold them to a local merchant, and he raised the price on them and sold them to the public. Also, we drank a lot of sassafras tea as kids growing up, which came from a tree root as well. It made the house smell so good. We sold all roots except for the tea root, and ginseng brought the most money out of any of them.

My dad and an uncle from my mom's family were working at the same place. Their employer had promoted my dad to foreman at a company that my uncle had worked at longer. Maybe some irritation was there for a time, but he still had to do what my father told him to do. Remembering this circumstance from when we were children helped us in our adult lives with moving through the ranks where we worked and adjusting others to our own authority. As children, we got to know all the other employees and the office staff as well. My father was a very respected worker, and I would say that is where I got my work ethic from.

My dad had several jobs throughout his life, from working on the local railways for a while to working with cranes at the last job he had. He would work two jobs at a time to make sure there was enough to provide for us. My grandfather (that is, the man who raised my mother) and my dad would work in the evenings and some weekends when they got behind in their work. My dad was never a lazy man.

When I was in the Brownies and Girl Scouts, I used to convince the bus driver in the summer to me drop me off where Dad worked, and I would sit in his truck or car, whatever he was driving at the time. I remember walking in, and he would get me a Tab or Fresca pop while he continued to work. It was amazing being a young girl and watching my father work for the money he made. I know some days he would be upset with me for getting off the bus there, but then in turn, he also knew I didn't want to be at home.

I was his sidekick. I would get greasy with him when he worked on automobiles for others on evenings and weekends, and even his own vehicles if needed. Our house was small when we moved two streets over, as it was only a two bedroom and one bath for all of us, but those bedrooms were big, and we shared.

At some points in his life, my dad would get so wasted and drunk, and he would be up at all hours of the night and yell at me to help him. I experienced what alcohol did to people, and I never wanted to get myself in a situation like what I had seen growing up (though that did not stop me from drinking—no, I did some throughout my life). I never regretted any of it, even if it meant I sat in the hallway and waited on him to get finished in the bathroom. As you can probably tell by reading this, I was a daddy's girl. I loved him very very much.

We had a neighbor who lived across the street, and he would get my dad to help him go deal with his cattle and do fence work if they got out. I was born on a farm, and I once got bucked by a ram as a child for not listening to my dad when we were out picking berries. It was early in the morning, and he asked me to go get him another cup of coffee, specifically telling me not to cut across the field. Well, I'd never seen the ram, so I thought I would be safe. My dad and older brother had to quit picking berries and come to my rescue. I could hear Dad saying, "It will kill you! Just be still, and we will get its attention, and then you get up and run very fast." I don't remember if I ran with the coffee cup or not—I just remember how frightened I was.

When we moved to the house in the country in the winter again—the house my parents rented from my aunt Elizabeth and uncle Al (the one who violated me), which you read about already—that was where I learned how to do carpentry work. Dad had to do a lot of work on the place just for us to live in it. So, with me he had me fetching his tools for his projects. I learned the names of tools and what they were used for. Proper operation was different for each tool, and you could get hurt very easily.

Back then, as we still live today, if any of my other siblings had listened to this advice or learned how to do things, I would get fewer calls. I help my family out with doing things because I have bought the tools needed to do many projects. Trust me, I am not complaining about helping them—helping your family is a great thing to do, because you get to spend time with them that you might not otherwise have gotten the chance to.

But sometimes my family will call and ask if they can borrow some of my tools. I allow them to use the tools, but sometimes the tools don't come back in an operative condition—and some were pricy, too. I have issues dealing with my family sometimes because they seemed to have fallen into another planet. We were all taught the same if you chose to learn it, but some of my siblings didn't want to take the advice of others in life at all and went down the wrong road.

In a family, everyone goes in a separate direction as they grow up, and that's okay, but you at least want to go forth in life and not stay in a rut. If you know any hot-headed people in your life, and you wonder why they continue to repeat the same old things and never learn from it, well, I have some of them in my life too. I guess you can't teach an old dog new tricks; they continue to fail out because they refuse to change their patterns. I only wish more of my family would know God or let God into their lives, because of the peace that comes with it and how your whole life changes.

I was devastated when my father passed away, because he was one of my rocks in life, along with my grandma. He was my savior from my mom when my grandma passed. But I do have a heavenly Father. I attended church as a child, though not all the time, because if Dad was going somewhere else on a Sunday, then I chose to go with him so I wasn't home with my mom all day. As a child, you learn in church, but not as much as it sets in as an adult, and when you put the teachings together, the puzzle falls into place. At such a young age, if you didn't attend church all the time, you really didn't know these things that we continue to learn each day in our lives. The things I have learned today have given me much more of an understanding as to how they fit into the world and my everyday life.

With my dad being so special to me, I could not tell him what happened at the hands of my uncle Al. I was twelve when this happened but he told me I was lying about my age because by arguing with me he said your fourteen. No matter what I said to my uncle Al he had a comeback about my age so I finally just stopped trying to prove myself. I knew I wasn't fourteen. I have always looked older than I was. My dad had been hurt in his late thirties when I was around ten or eleven because I was still in elementary school by his nephew, who hit him in the back of the head with a two-by-four. That crushed his skull, and he was in the hospital for over thirty days having skull reconstruction. My dad lost his hearing on the recovery table waking up, which changed our lives forever. It affected his speech, and I was the only person who could understand him after his surgery.

This happened in the 1970s and my aunt Tonya (my dad's sister) wanted my mother to press charges against my cousin Jim. My mom did not want to do anything, even though my dad's sister Tonya was willing to take on paying the lawyer fee, so my cousin was never charged for this. Some might wonder why and how the law charges some people for what they do to others, and yet others get by hurting others without any consequences.

Mother never did adhere to any advice, and from then on, my father's side of the family had no use for her. I was the go-to person to relay what he was saying. I was able to spend more and more time with him—not that I didn't feel like I was his favorite, but he taught me so much in life. Dad's speech improved some over the years, but he never could hear again. They offered him sign language and he turned it down, saying he was too old. How funny, because he was only in his late thirties, but I understood where he was coming from—we had already adapted some of our own sign language with him. I applied everything he taught me to my life today and yesterday, so I know he was proud of me.

When my father died of COPD and heart failure, it was in May of 2003. Why did this happen in the same season as everything else in my life? Is there a pattern or not, or maybe a reason? He was a very well-known man throughout the community, and it was so nice to see many people we had forgotten as kids when they attended his funeral. We grew up knowing who they were and forgot some of their names, but they never forgot who we were—our names may have slipped their minds, but not our faces.

My father's family would say he was their favorite uncle, and I can really see why, because he taught them a lot in life. My cousin who hurt my father said he regretted what he did, and if he could have taken it back, he would have not done it. A family goes through things in life, and we really need to step back and access the situations before doing something we will regret in the future. My cousin said he was paying dearly for what he had done to his uncle—and he did suffer from one thing after another until cancer finally took him away from everyone.

As we grow up, we can see both rejection and reflection being a part of how we feel at any age, and we might wonder about the "what if" and the "why" of what went on and how we try and get through it in our lives. Letting others control your life is not something I got from my dad. He never let anything someone said or did bother him. On the other hand, I was not pleasant with people when I knew things were being said to me or about me that were not true. I was bold enough to say my peace and keep my feet grounded with others. I would apologize if I had done wrong but would tell you in a split second, "Hold up, you don't know what you're talking about," without batting an eye.

Reflections

In your life, who impacted you the most in terms of overcoming obstacles?

_____
_____
_____
_____
_____
_____
_____
_____
_____
_____
_____
_____
_____
_____
_____
_____
_____
_____

CHAPTER FIVE

Rejection

Some may say rejection is only how you feel, but sometimes that is not necessary so. The turns our life takes as we grow play a major factor in our mentality. I can speak from experience that the things that happen to you in life can interfere with your mind.

I know some of you reading this can understand what feeling like an outcast from your friends and family is like. I took it as a normal thing because as I grew up, I became much angrier the older I got. If I was called a Bitch, I would go after that person and deal with them. Anger is not a good thing. People should respect others before jumping in and doing such horrible things to them without knowing their story, because you can really come out on the wrong side if they flip out on you, which I did.

The negativity I went through in life made me that type of person. The things that had been acceptable weren't anymore, and it became quite noticeable to everyone. The law was called on me many times as a teen because of the nonsense that I refused to tolerate. If I was not carrying so much on myself as a kid, it might not have bothered me like it did. I just wonder how others felt, knowing that they walked around with the baggage at any stage of their life where nothing seemed to work out.

Being rejected by my mother hurt really badly, so I had to put up a defense mechanism to get through life around her. My cousins told me how my grandmother would make me climb in behind her sick body so my mother would not harm me. I hated that more and more as I grew up. All I ever had known was that, no matter what, she hated me. That wall I put up also played tricks on my mind: it was hard going day to day throughout my life hating her. After my grandmother passed, the years just continued to get worse between me and my mother. I was always getting the blame for all her issues, or at least that's how it has always seemed to me. Maybe if she had treated me like a daughter, like a human being, those thoughts would not have been what they were.

Another one of my aunts, who was married to my dad's brother, didn't like how I dressed or acted. She called me a bitch and said that I would have lots of kids and live off the government welfare system. I would love for her to see me today. I was not the person she thought I was—her interpretation of me was so wrong. As it turns out, I have no children. That was not in my plans but God's plan for me, but it shows that she really didn't know me. The person she reminded me of was my mom, except that she never judged her own kids. They lived as adults at my grandpa's house just like she did. She had kids who had kids and were living off the system, but I guess that was okay for them. I even told her that I was not going to have kids and live off welfare, and I have stayed true to that statement.

I was rejected by men for being too independent. But I was taught to take care of myself and guard myself from all that had happened to me all those years ago. I know I didn't fit in with others because of the way I grew up. Living poor has its up and downs in life. If you grow up poor, you cherish what you have much more. When life goes well, you become more confident in yourself, but the thoughts are still running in the background that you're not worthy to be a part of things or good enough to hang with certain people.

What I have found, though, is that the older I get, the more I think and wonder how those who thought they had it all together in the past have lost that mindset as they grow older. Life does throw us curve balls, and what we do with it defines us.

People can be so cruel even to ourselves at times. We all need to reflect on our attitudes on a daily basis, and we also need to decipher our actions as to how others are treating us. We can love and hate at the same time—though "hate" is such a strong word, and we should try using "dislike" instead. We should love with all our hearts, not based on our own thoughts as we may think of someone, or our ideal or a perception of someone based on how they look or talk or walk. We should be more like Jesus, recognizing that we are all alike and are loved just the same.

No matter what we experience in life, we all have to give up something. What would that be in your life—your siblings or other family members? Or maybe even yourself, always sacrificing your happiness to try and appease others. Always trying to fit in with others at school or family functions. We all want to be accepted, so why sacrifice your own self or your life?

GOD'S PATHWAY

Have you ever felt rejection? If so, when did this happen, and what was your outcome?

CHAPTER SIX

Sacrificing

Let me begin by asking this: what have you sacrificed in life? How about your own life to care for others, whether related to you or not? Or you may have sacrificed a job, friends, family, or anything else you can think of. I think we have all sacrificed something in our lives. I would include not being selfish as a form of sacrifice.

Sacrificing yourself growing up and into adulthood, you lose that ability to connect with others, which makes me feel that is one reason

why I felt all that rejection. When I felt rejected, I got lost in all areas of life, maybe because I had been sacrificing my time for my family and making sure they were cared for. It could also have been because of how I felt about being violated at such a young age.

My mother passed when I was twenty, in the early 1980s. It could have been the cruel intentions of her actions to many of us as we grew up that she wanted us to suffer more now by watching such a horrific situation. My dad said he could take care of the boys, and asked me if I could raise my sister. You might ask, why he wouldn't care for her too? Well, he was not her real dad, but he raised her as his own.

My younger sister was about to turn ten shortly after our mother's passing, and I really had my own personal issues with her. The hatred I had for my mom really got in the way because my youngest sister's breath smelled like my mother's. Our mother had babied her with everything like she was the only child she ever had. Of course, I had given my input to my mom about how she was raising her not to be independent for herself, but let's just say she was catered to. My dad continued to care for the younger boys, with my help, of course.

It all seemed like a dream, being on my own and still caring for everyone. I always thought I would be having a life someday. My younger half-sister left my home at the age of nineteen. She went to live with some friends and was able to get a job. She returned to Dad's house and had a baby, and with Dad becoming more ill, I told her that since she was staying under his roof, she could keep an eye on him for me. But then I got phone calls from the law saying she had left her child alone in the house, knowing my dad was not well enough to care for an infant, especially since she left the child in a room upstairs and my dad could not hear.

Well, my father's health took a turn for the worse, and I had to take him in as my job required me to worked twelve-hour shifts. During this time of caring for my father and often my younger sister's kids too, I had to call my other siblings for help with Dad. I knew the time had come for me to call the other four kids and ask them to help watch him because of my work schedule. My request was for each of them to have him for 24 hours, and I would take him on my days off because I always took him to his appointments. Well, as it turned out, I didn't get any help from them. My younger brother would try and get him once a week, but that was it. My younger sister told me she couldn't because she had her own family. She would only help once in a while to take him to his appointments if I was forced to work overtime.

One day, while Dad was waiting on my younger brother to come get him, he fell and busted his head open. He always had my younger brother's phone number just in case something happened. My sister-in-law answered the phone, and she told my brother, "I think that was your dad. I think you need to go check on him." Let me tell you, I've had lots of turns and twists in my life, and it was not always a roller coaster journey I wanted to ride. Of course, I was pulling a twelve-hour day at work when I got the phone call: "What am I to do with dad? He hurt his head and had been bleeding." I said, "Take him to urgent care. I am on my way as soon as I get ahold of my boss."

When I made it to the urgent care center, I asked all those questions: "Why did you not show up when you said you would? You know he paces until you get him if you give him a time." My dad was just so happy to get out of the house and spend time with his kids. He couldn't drive because of his health—that was a chore in itself when I told him he couldn't drive and the Bureau of Motor Vehicles sent him a card telling him it was past time to get his driver's license renewed. That was a war for a while, because he just didn't understand why they would send it to him if he couldn't drive. Let me just say I picked that choice for him because of his health; I didn't want him or anyone else to be in danger.

The reality of all this is that the help he needed was not there for him. But if Dad was admitted into the hospital and they could not understand what he was saying, or he couldn't understand what they were doing, someone had to be there around the clock as much as possible. I got the help needed for that from my younger brother. He was a sweetheart; he would spend his nights at the hospital. We worked my dad's stay around our hours of work: it might be me in the evening and my brother during the day, depending on our work schedules. The hospital had our numbers if neither of us could be there because we were both at work. Some sacrificed more than others with my dad.

My dad started to need some more required care, so I had to put him in a nursing home. I hated every minute of it, but I had no other choice because of my work schedule. During one of my few days off, he asked to come home, so I agreed to let him come for the night. This wasn't the easiest task to complete. He was weak and used a wheelchair to get around. The nursing home allowed me to borrow it to help. I got him home and we managed to get him inside, but not without obstacles in our way. We both went down with the wheelchair, and when I got up, I sat Dad up, then the chair, and then tried again to move him inside. Well, I couldn't get him and the chair up the steps. I sat him on the porch, brought the wheelchair to the porch, and then tried to get him to the chair, but we didn't get there. I couldn't get him to his feet, so I had to pull him to the front door and into the house. Then, between the both of us, we were able to get him back into the wheelchair and into his chair at the house. I think he was seeing if I had just left him and gotten rid of his belongings and such, including his room.

It was time to get him ready for bed. At that time, I didn't know the nursing home had him in diapers; I assumed he just didn't need to go. So, when I realized this, I had to run to town and get them and head back home, leaving him by himself, but I knew he wasn't going to move because he was too weak and worn out. Being a daughter, you never would think you would have to help your father in that way. The next morning, we got up and changed him again, got him fed, and he said, "Sis, it's time to take me back."

He passed in 2003, not long after his visit to the house. I think he knew it was too much for me. My whole world changed after that happened. In the fall of 2004 I broke my left foot and needed a cast, and thirty days later I was in a horrible car crash.

As a result, I was let go from my job. I was given the choice between a disability retirement or taking a penalty for three years' probation, where if I did anything wrong, they would walk me to the gate. I took the disability retirement, and my boss wasn't happy with me. I said, "Why would I allow someone to judge me for something, and if anything went wrong, too bad for me?" He said, "You know what you are doing and do it well." But when other bosses had issues with people, they got fired, and I knew with all my heart I was one of them.

During the process of getting approved for disability outside my job, I just about lost my house too. This was during the time when Barack Obama was president and the government created the Home Affordable Refinance Program so people would not lose their homes due to the economy. I filled out all the necessary paperwork and qualified, but that didn't stop the bank from trying to take my home. My brother called and asked why my house was on the market, and I said it wasn't. Then I received paperwork from the bank that they were going to do a short sale on my home.

I took the letter to an attorney in my town, and he said the bank could do that because even though that program was put in place, there some banks did not understand what the program process really meant. So, the lawyer told me I needed to have it paid before the end of the next day at 4pm. Thank God, I remembered I had a 401k, and I called to have them send me enough money to pay this and overnight the check to me. I had to drive two hours to pay it after I received the check from my 401k plan. I made it at 3:55pm, just before Wells Fargo was closing their doors for the day. I saw many people in that office who were trying to save their homes and weren't as fortunate as I was. Some had already lost theirs, per the program. I contacted the state attorney general's office, and they told me the bank I went through was one of the ones that were not following directions. I could see them making lots of money from me because I owed less than $50,000. and my house was appraised at over $250,000. So that put me right back into a bind with my bills.

I have sacrificed a lot during my life with family, work, and companies of many. That roller coaster presents many obstacles in my life, and many roads are still less traveled. But I am so glad I have a mighty God on my side who has helped me throughout my walk in life.

I still continue to help my family. I am a guardian to two nephews who have different disabilities, because I know that someone has to care for those who cannot care for themselves. They have support people who help them, and that is a blessing of its own. It gives me some much-needed time to get things done or just to rest. I have many things going on in my life today that end up being a challenge, to say the least, but I keep on trucking forward with the help of my heavenly Father who hasn't let me down.

Some might think that they would have someone to fall back on in times of need. I can speak for myself and say that no matter what you do for others, the same isn't given back. My sister just understood me when I started to need more help, she was there for me. I understand that others have lives to live, but so did I, and I do now. What I haven't figured out along this journey is, where is the respect one should show for others? I have always felt alone and like I don't fit in or meet up to their expectations of being good enough. How would you feel if after all that you have done for your family, you still felt like an outcast?

I almost had to give up in my childhood and my teenage years. I'm not saying that I didn't get to do some fun things with friends, but more often, that was not so. It makes me wonder why I chose to do what I did, but I sit and think, who would have if I hadn't? People's bitterness can outweigh some things in life. While doing all I did, I would and could not tell my dad what had happened to me at a young age, as I knew the repercussions that would have taken place with my dad not living the life outside of bars. My father, being the man he was, did not deserve any more of a miserable life than he had already endured by my mother and cousin's actions, and many others I don't even know about. How does the pain of sacrificing yourself impact you later on in life. What are you doing to yourself by allowing what has happened to consume you?

Reflections

Have you ever sacrificed for something or someone, or are you still sacrificing something today? How did that feel? Are there some changes you can make to change what you're sacrificing? Does it allow you to feel good or bad about what you are doing?

_____

_____

_____

_____

_____

_____

_____

_____

_____

_____

_____

_____

_____

_____

_____

_____

GOD'S PATHWAY

Reflections

CHAPTER SEVEN

Desire of Living

I allowed the hurt and the world to consume me. Why? I always wondered that too, until one day, I woke up to the possibility that there was more to this life than what I had ever experienced. We have to be vulnerable by having an ear to listen to what we can hear in silence. Our heavenly Father is the masterpiece of this world and when we can come to grips with how it all takes place, will we ever be able to come along in harmony with ourselves and others?

Peace is letting go of all those despairs in life that we take to heart on almost a daily basis. When others give us a compliment, how do we really accept it? Some people, perhaps because of what their roller coaster is like in life, do not know how to accept a compliment, or even know what that word really means. The Merriam-Webster dictionary defines the verb "to compliment" as "to express esteem, respect, affection, or admiration to."

I know for me, it's hard because of the past that I endured. I hate that I feel this way, because some people are not so genuine in the things they say to you. The process has to be deciphered, even though we cross paths with it on a daily basis with others—it's about knowing what you feel and how to freely accept what is being said at the time.

I have often been asked, "Why do you have a hard time accepting a compliment or not realize it was a compliment to start with?" If I could figure this part out, it would help me to smile more and know that what was said to me was genuine. But to take you a little further, I could not even tell you if someone was actually flirting with me. I feel embarrassed when I get called out on it. If I had not grown up the way I did, I might have been normal in some situations that others just pick up on very fast.

Joy comes in the morning when we wake up from our peaceful rest that is given us. Give thanks every day for what you have or don't have, because material things come and go, but the love of Jesus stays forever. I am happy I got the opportunity to experience life in so many different areas, because if I hadn't, I might not be able to reach others in the way God has shown me throughout life. We don't all learn the same things in life—for example, I became well rounded in many different aspects of things such as gardening, working on automobiles, and knowing how to hunt for different kinds of roots in the woods.

Keep in mind that we remember and see things differently based on how we experienced life growing up. I sit and think of the world today and how people are taught. Why has the world changed so much? Most people hate change, but there are many things they haven't had the chance to experience because their parents or caretakers were never shown or taught these things in life. How do you survive in the world with the teachings you got growing up? What can you do if you have to survive without money? Can you be productive in growing a garden, living off the earth for what you can eat if you had to, knowing some of these things can help you if ever you get lost in the wilderness?

Today's world comes from easy and fast, but for me, the reality of life is that I was taught the hard things of survival so that if I had to rely on what I was taught, I could provide. I started out growing up with money, but it got harder as other siblings came along. We learned how to adapt to running out of things, but then I learned what it was like to lose that money. I have always been able to adapt to the ups and downs in life. Were things easy as a kid, teenager, or adult? Not without compromise.

I want to say that if things seem to have gotten off track in your life, in whatever season or reason, keep your head up and listen for direction, because it will definitely be worth it. What a journey we have traveled through—and the journey still continues. Don't think for a minute that I didn't come out on top of a messy roller coaster. Destruction comes in many forms in our lives, and we have to continue to move forward. We have to make the decision not to let things hold us back or tear us down. Can we stop destroying ourselves and come out the winner?

The choices we make definitely have a big impact on our lives. Are you willing to make the change of letting go of the negative that has occurred in your life? Are the steps to letting it go greater than what we shall see as we move forward?

Reflections

Have you ever made a decision about how to live your life? If so, what did look it like, or what changed your thoughts?

GOD'S PATHWAY
Reflections

CHAPTER EIGHT

Letting Go of My Mother

When I was eighteen and had to bring everything out about my uncle Al, he decided that since my parents were renting from them, this caused a problem for me and for them. I had graduated from high school at this point and had a part-time job. I returned home from work one evening and all hell broke loose. I entered the house and my mom said I had to move out, and I asked, "Why?" Who would have thought that he would stoop to that level and tell my parents that if I didn't move out, they all had to move out? I went into my room and shut the door. My mother told my dad that I had an issue with what my uncle Al. So my mother wrote dad a note and told him that I was refusing to go. I retreated to my room to try and figure out why she would sit there and not want to stand up for me with him. Was I letting that destruction settle back in, still harboring old feelings?

My father had been drinking, which changed his demeanor with me too. I could see a look in his eyes that I hadn't seen before, so the thought of all this was hurtful to me. He busted down the door to my door. I know he didn't know what was happening because I could not tell him what happened to me when I was a kid—if I had told him, my uncle would not have been standing there that day, my dad being disabled or not. But I know that if my dad had known the situation, things would not have gone this way.

I was calling a few people to help me leave. My boyfriend finally showed up and we were leaving, and my dad got his gun and started firing shots and yelling at us. I was told to leave, so I was just doing what I was told to do. The pain I felt was so unreal—why didn't she just tell me instead of getting my dad involved with me having to move out? Believing it could have been handled so differently than it was puzzled me. I knew my dad was feeling some kind of guilt, but this would never have happened if he had just known what happened to me.

I had to call the law because he damaged my boyfriend's car and it was Labor Day weekend, and they charged him and sent him to jail. That made me even more angry because I could not bring myself to tell him what happened, but he knew I loved him until the day he passed on. When my dad got out of jail the next day, I went and picked him up, and he was not mad at me. I know he really didn't understand why my uncle Al was doing this, and he told me he was sorry. We pulled up in front of the house and found that my stuff was in a tent on Grandpa's property. My dad asked why I was in the tent and I wrote down as to what mom said my uncle Al said and refreshed his memory of what took place that night. My grandpa's property boundaries lines connected up with my uncle Al property. He showed up and started running his mouth about where my tent was placed, and my grandpa put him in his place. I laughed at my uncle Al when Grandpa told him to remove his well off his property. My uncle remembered, "Oh yes, that is on your land." The well supplied water to his house. My grandpa had asked why I was doing all this before my dad was released from jail and I had told him.

My grandpa told him to stop what he was doing to the family and that his son should not have gone to jail with his conditions. Now, as you have read, not many knew what had happened to me, just those who needed to know. Had my mother done what she should have done when I was a kid, this would already have been dealt with years prior.

I ran an electric cord to the tent for light. This was in September, so the weather was only getting colder, which had its challenges. I was only part time at my job, and I bought food for the family when there was no money, so it took me until January of the following year to save up enough money to rent a small apartment. It wasn't anything fancy, but better to be cold inside a building than a tent made of canvas. I survived, as you know, or this book would not have come to be. Like a roller coaster, you never know where you are going unless you have ridden it before.

I paid the rent and the landlord let me make payments for the deposit. I lived there a few months without heat, but it was still better than what I had just come from. I know my dad hated what was going on, but he also knew I was smart enough to understand he couldn't afford anything more than what he was paying for rent. They all needed a roof over their heads too, and he had to look after the young kids still at home.

We would not have had to rent if Mom had just

purchased the house in town with dad's severance pay all those years ago. Yet had my mother made that choice not to buy the house, things would have been so different for the whole entire family, and she was the one who made that decision, not my father. They were going to sell my parents the house for $5,000, which was a lot of money in the seventies, but we would not have had to move. During the time it took for my parents to find a place for us to move into, I went and lived in a different school district with another aunt and uncle on my dad's side of family.

While my dad was in the hospital, we spent too much time with my mom's side of the family. I was enrolled into another school while with them, and they were told that after thirty days, they would have to adopt me in order for me to continue to go there. Well, guess what—Mom would not allow them to do that. I had to return to live with them. Back to the life I hated. It always boiled down to money with her.

Once I had an apartment, my mom never visited when my dad would bring the other siblings over when they didn't have anything to eat. My father was very caring; it was cheaper for him to borrow gas money to bring them to my house to eat than to buy food for their house.

One day in the spring, which seems to be the season when everything happens in my life, there was a knock at the door, and I saw her standing there with my dad. I asked what was going on because she had never come to my house until that day, and I got the news that my grandpa had just died. She was there a whopping five minutes, if that, then went back to the truck; Dad stayed a while. It was a sad day because my grandpa had stood up to my uncle on behalf of our family.

Time moved on, and I was working a full-time job, which helped me get another place to live after I was told I had to move because they had sold the place that I was renting. But the bills were higher at the house I was now renting, and still being a true newbie at this renting stuff made it harder to stay in the house rather than an apartment. I had to start looking for an apartment or a cheaper house to rent.

During this time after my move to the new house I rented, my mother had been diagnosed with cancer. After Mom was told she had to go to another town for treatment, her family called me up and told me, "You need to come out to the house." I had to borrow a car to get there because I walked to work. When I arrived, my aunt Goldie told me that I needed to spend more time at the house to help out with my siblings and clean the house. Well, you know, she never came around and did anything, and I reminded her of that. I told her she had no right to tell me what to do, but she didn't know what my uncle had made me do, like sleep in a tent in the winter. Of course, they had plenty of money but never offered to help us out, or even her. So, did they really think that after everything that happened in this house where they lived, I would ever think about cleaning it up, since I wasn't supposed to be there anyway?

I did let it all go, even with the expectations of what her family said to me. She went to her appointment with the other doctor, and I never got a straight answer; all I knew is it was not good. She later died of ovarian cancer, which was uncurable at that time, at the age of thirty-eight. The day she passed, she was at home, and all the kids were there but me. When the squad arrived at the house, they wanted to take her to the hospital, but she refused. She just asked them to roll her onto her stomach, knowing she didn't have the strength to anything for herself. She must have been in so much pain, she just didn't care what impact it was going to have on my younger siblings. They watched her face go into the pillow, and after a few minutes, they rolled her over and she had passed away with her head in the pillow. My brother and sisters told me about what they did, and I was upset that they did that and let my siblings watch.

Now that we are at this point in the story, I can tell you that it never stopped with this aunt Dottie. At the funeral home, I was asked why I was not crying. Now we all know not everyone grieves the same, but what she didn't know when she judged me for how I was acting was the emotional roller coaster I had lived with my mother. I was there for my father and siblings, no one else. Some years later, the aunt Dottie and uncle Sam did finally purchase her a headstone, but not until my dad had passed, even though they knew he would never be able to afford one for her. But I am sure my uncle Al hated to see her go, because he always made sure she had food to eat and money.

One day when I was a kid, we had no food in the house, and my uncle Al was at the other house below ours. I went through my mom's purse and found over forty dollars. I took the money, and when she came back, I had already showed Dad and we were going to the town to get food. She was mad, but so were we all. Children shouldn't do things like get into an adult's purse, but the lies of this woman made me sick. My uncle AL always gave her food, and she got to eat regardless of us kids—how wrong was that! My belief is that my younger sister belonged to him and that was one of his ways of keeping it quiet. My aunt Elizabeth may have thought this too but had no real proof but my sister looked a lot like her other children.

As you see, I wasn't the best daughter in the world, but I was not the worst kid either. I always wondered why she despised me so much all my life, and this is still a mystery to me. I can only think of how I suffered with all this negativity in my life after leaving the nest. I have wondered how my life would have turned out had my dad picked the other lady to marry instead of my mom. I may never have been born, I don't know, but Dad had always talked about the other lady many times while I was growing up. I still have not met her, but I hope to someday, just to see her demeanor with others, including myself. Not that it matters today, but I guess it's just something on my bucket list.

When you have conversations with others, you learn more about how their lives are similar to or different from yours. Have you ever thought about how you let go of someone or something? We continue to let things consume us for all different reasons and seasons, and truly letting go of something that has just been killing you inside and out for years is the most painful thing to adjust to. But the most rewarding is when you never have to think again about that person who has consumed you for over forty years.

Reflections

Have you ever made a change in a relationship with someone and made peace with that person? How did that affect what happened or help you make those circumstances come full circle?

CHAPTER NINE

Moving Forward

When I was able to understand what my life was going to be like, I felt like I should have tried to figure this out a long time ago. But if you're not right in your walk in life, you will have trouble understanding why things happen to you the way they do.

I have seen many therapists and psychologists over the course of my life, who tried many treatments to figure out what I might need to help me adjust to all the abuse. Not feeling the love of my mother or understanding why she did those things was still holding on to me even as an adult, and I needed to try and move forward in my life. The medication that they suggest one takes for this either works or it doesn't, but it is a process, as some of you reading this may know.

Carrying that baggage with you throughout your life is a burden to the one person it affects, and that would be you yourself. Freedom is given to us each and every day—we just have to seek it. So, I have a simple question for you to ask yourself: is there something you're holding on to, something that you find to be carrying you and you can't seem to let it go? If so, I would suggest you give it over to your heavenly Father, and he will walk with you during any storm, no matter the situation. It just took me many years before I was able to go after what I needed and get that peace in my life.

When you are advised not to take your past into any new relationships, it really does seem impossible when the people you are with act in ways that remind you of what you experienced before. But the way to handle it depends on how you deal with it on a personal level. Earlier in this book, I shared with you the fact that I was violated as a kid. I really wondered if anyone believed me when I would tell them of my situation as a kid growing up, until I was in a relationship with a man for around ten years. One day he touched me and out of my mouth came the words "Would you please stop groping me?" He said, "I am not doing that." Even as an adult, I didn't know what that word meant or how it applied to what was happening at that time. It came out of nowhere, and I said I was sorry.

Even when we think we don't have triggers that make us relive our past, or we think we are over something that goes deep inside, it can still pop out of nowhere when you least expect it. I have always thought people should not engage with other people who don't know them and have no clue what they have endured in life. From my own personal experience, I am going to tell you about a situation I was in and let you think about how it is that stuff can come out of nowhere.

I was invited by a friend to come over and eat because he knew what I had been going through. When he called me, I refused for a while, but then gave in and agreed to go eat a little. But honestly, I couldn't eat—it was more that we engaged in conversation. You might be wondering how this pertains to my story, but he was the one I was with for those years I explained earlier. I was about to leave, but he asked me not to, so I stayed until it started to get dark out. His phone kept ringing and I told him to answer it, but he said he didn't want to talk to the lady who was calling. I pleaded with him, but he refused. Then she showed up while I was there, so I said it was time to leave. I got up and gave him a hug, and then she grabbed me by the hair and it snapped me. I blacked out and didn't know where I was or what I was doing, only to say that I in the state if mind I was in I just wanted to pounce her head off the oak trim but had no idea any of this was going on. I was in a different state of mind at this time. After coming out from the blackout spell I went into is what my mother did to me as a child. It put me into a state of mind of not having any idea of what was really going on between the two of us. I don't even remember engaging into a confrontational with this lady at all. It goes to show this does happen to people and is a real condition that is not made up.

By the time I came out of that spell from the past, I cried because I was so ashamed this had happened. I took myself into another room and got myself together, or so I thought, then left without saying anything. This person had tried to remove me off her and couldn't do so, but that didn't leave me without bruises from his force on me. So please, as I say this, just remember that if you have a past like mine, you never know what will trigger something from the past or when it will show itself.

Being invited to attend a ladies' group and doing some Bible studies has helped me more than any doctor. I allowed myself to be vulnerable and honest with myself as I participated in doing the many workbooks to allow myself freedom.

I was involved in a horrible accident that has created a lot of obstacles in my life. I lost my job due to disabilities and head trauma with short and long-term memory loss. As the years have continued, I have been diagnosed with many other life-altering ailments as well. They say a cat has nine lives—if you believe that, well, I wonder how many lives I get a chance at because of all the near life-altering incidents that could have taken place in my life. I do believe it wasn't my time, that my heavenly Father has more for me to complete before my time is up on this earth.

Most of the major issues in my life seem to happen in the springtime. How do we adjust and let that season set in and present itself in our daily life moving forward? The adjustment is different, for sure, but in reality, did everything that ever happened to you in life happen in one season or many seasons of your daily life.

Reflections

Has there ever been a time when you had to move on from a situation? If so, How was that process and the effects it had on you? Did you seek help or need support, and if so, how did that work out for you?

_____

_____

_____

_____

_____

_____

_____

_____

_____

_____

_____

_____

_____

_____

_____

CHAPTER TEN

Seasons

How do the seasons affect your situation as they come and go? If you find that this is a learning time, you can't just sit back and wait for your favorite season to come around. We would all like it to be about seventy-five to seventy-seven degrees all the time—or maybe if you live in an area cold with cold winters, you look forward to the snow. But we all know that the seasons always change, and what was cold will become warm again.

Truly the new beginnings of life are so awesome to watch. It's so fascinating to watch all the dead trees and plants rebloom in spring. The colors are just so beautiful. I love traveling to see the world and how others live. I am fascinated with all the different areas of the world and what they have that other places don't have.

The trees budding and the new leaves, or the leaves falling to the ground and dying for their sleep time, as I would say, give time for rebirth. We all need to rebirth ourselves so that we don't allow the ugly or dirtiness to get us put under the rug, as some would say. Life's struggles are real for anyone who has undergone traumatic circumstances. Depression and PTSD are real, pain is real, and why people have to judge others is so beyond me.

We have all struggled with life circumstances in many different seasons. Our challenges may not all be the same, but each of us should have a good friend or two who invests time in us as we would for them. I know I take time out for others, sometimes putting myself on the back burner. Maybe the reason I do such things is that I don't want to be like others. I know that I have made a difference in people's lives because of my compassion and respect for others' feelings. The different things we learn in life helps others in their struggles and it gives them a sense of hope to move forward.

Most of us know that a roller coaster ride can be rough and bumpy. We first have to get in line and wait, and the excitement and fear set in, but the anticipation can either be rewarding or lead to discouragement. As we go up the hill and come down, that's life—we live that roller coaster. Some parts of our seasons have twists and turns that are more fearful and bothersome than others. The ride finishes, as do our seasons, and a new one begins. When the ride is finished, there's a question of what we thought of that roller coaster and what lesson we learned from the feel of the ride that we completed. When the roller coaster has finally stopped, we realize we either want to stay on it or move forward.

It's time to get real with yourself—whether the world we live in is good, bad, or ugly, we need to put ourselves first sometimes. Of course, our heavenly Father comes first, then us, because without God, we are nothing. I pray you are a believer, but if not, I make no judgment on you. But I want you to know that no matter your circumstances, someone really does care about you and for you. You may not feel it all the time, but trust me as I say this, I do, even though you don't know me personally.

Just to give one example, I told someone I was writing a book, and her response shocked me—as soon as I said the word "book," she went into telling me a little about her life, which I hadn't even asked her about, and I was beyond amusement. Talking to her, I made a comment, "Well, if I ever get my book written or published, I'll have to share it with you." She is such a nice doctor (though she isn't my doctor), and she just always resonates with a smile and is so willing to help others. She even mentioned getting me to sign it! I smiled and laughed, and I said that if I was ever to become famous, she would have a signed book. I said I really didn't think that would happen, but I would surely sign it if that was her wish.

You never know whose path you might come across that just saying "Hi" or "How are you?" makes someone's day. A simple conversation with them may save their life, because they might feel just as I did while growing up. Seasons change all the time, so stuff can change for a person at any moment. We are all human and we make mistakes. We are not perfect and never will be, and sometimes we will fail ourselves. It's not about being perfect, it's about what we make of our seasons and how we adapt to the changing times.

Forgive those who have done you wrong for whatever reason. The freedom it gives to your soul is great. Don't be deceived by what you can or can't see, because justice is something we all deserve to have in our lives.

A roller coaster, whether short or long, is always fun if you enjoy that time of adventure. Yes, they are scary, but a lot of things in life truly are until you do it once or twice. Rely on your instincts, because those hilly rides can make you sick, but only if you allow it. But an upset ride really tears at your stomach with nerves or something like fear.

Remember, your life can change no matter what season you seem to have gone through. You have people who care and will listen to you. Seek your heavenly Father for direction. If you don't know him, I pray you can find a church that is right for you and seek those in it for help. Please take the steps to move forward and not sit still and let something become a stronghold or bondage in life.

Reflections

If you have tried it your own way, how was that experience? Did it work out for you?

Have you ever thought about seeking God for help before that difficult season? Have you tried seeking him for his guidance? If not, why not? Would you consider it?

_____

_____

_____

_____

_____

_____

_____

_____

_____

_____

_____

_____

_____

_____

This was given to me as a statement piece that we can go forth knowing. Give it some thought as you read it, because it is so true.

"*Because He lives,*

I can face tomorrow,

Because He lives,

all fear is gone;

Because I know He holds the future,

And life is worth the living,

Just because He lives!"

Chorus from Bill Gaither's song "Because He Lives"
GOD REVEALS THE PICTURE OF YOUR PATH.

www.ingramcontent.com/pod-product-compliance
Lightning Source LLC
LaVergne TN
LVHW021619080426
835510LV00019B/2662